THE BASICS OF SEO

Master the Art of Ranking High and Boosting Traffic

Ray Goodwin

CONTENTS

LIABILITY DISCLAIMER

The information contained within this book is intended for informational purposes only and should not be construed as legal or professional advice. The authors and publishers of this book are not responsible for any losses or damages that may arise from the use of the information contained within.

The reader assumes full responsibility for any decisions made based on the information in this book. The authors and publishers do not endorse any particular method, service or product mentioned in this book and are not responsible for any consequences resulting from their use.

The reader should exercise caution and discretion when making life changing decisions, and should be aware of the risks and potential consequences of their actions. This book is not a substitute for professional or legal advice and should not be relied upon as such.

By reading and using the information in this book, the reader acknowledges and agrees to hold harmless the authors, publishers, and any other parties involved in the creation or distribution of this book from any and all liability, claims, damages, or losses that may arise from their use of the information contained herein.

CHAPTER 1: INTRODUCTION TO SEO

Welcome to The Basics of SEO, a comprehensive guide to understanding the fundamentals of search engine optimization. As someone who has spent over 25 years in the online sales industry, I have seen first-hand how critical it is for businesses to have a strong online presence. One of the key ways to achieve this is through effective SEO.

In this book, I aim to demystify SEO and break it down into easy-to-understand concepts that anyone can learn and implement. Whether you are a small business owner looking to improve your website's visibility or an aspiring digital marketer wanting to sharpen your skills, this book will provide you with the foundation you need to succeed.

Throughout these pages, I will cover everything from keyword research and on-page optimization techniques to link building strategies and measurement tools. But beyond just tactics and tips, I will also explore the larger principles that underpin successful SEO campaigns – such as user experience, content quality, and ethical practices.

So if you're ready to ramp up your online visibility and drive more traffic, sales, and leads, then let's get started!

Overview

In today's digital age, businesses need an online presence to thrive in the market. However, having a website isn't enough. You need to make sure your website is easily discoverable by search engines such as Google, Bing, and Yahoo. This is where Search Engine Optimization (SEO) comes into play.

SEO is the practice of optimizing websites to rank higher in organic search results. Organic results refer to the web pages that appear in the results pages due to their relevance to the search term entered by the user. A higher ranking in organic search results leads to more visibility and traffic to your website, which can eventually lead to more revenue.

The concept of SEO has been around for over two decades since the rise of search engines in the 1990s. The earliest search engines such as Archie, Gopher, and Yahoo relied on human-powered directories to categorize websites. However, with the rise of Google in the late '90s, the concept of using algorithms to rank websites based on keywords and backlinks became the norm.

Today, SEO is essential for businesses of all sizes and niches. With over 3.5 billion Google searches per day, ranking higher in search results means being seen by potential customers, which can lead to more revenue and growth for your business.

There are two types of search results: organic and paid. Organic search results refer to the natural results that appear as searched terms in the search engine. They're ranked based on various factors such as relevance, authority, and user experience, and they're not paid for by businesses. On the other hand, paid search results are sponsored ads that appear at the top of the search engine results pages, and businesses pay for them.

Search engines use complex algorithms to rank web pages based on various factors such as the relevance to the search terms, the quality of content and backlinks, and the user experience. These are called search engine ranking factors, and they are constantly evolving as search engines strive to provide the most relevant results for their users.

There are three types of searches: navigational, informational, and transactional. Navigational searches are when people search for a specific website or page, such as "Facebook login page." Informational searches are when people search for information on a specific topic, such as "how to make pizza dough." Transactional searches are when people search with the intent to purchase or take action, such as "buy iPhone 12."

SEO best practices refer to the techniques and strategies used to optimize websites for search engines. They include keyword research, on-page optimization, backlinking, and technical optimization.

However, there are many misconceptions about SEO, such as the belief that it is a one-time task or that it involves "tricking" search engines. In reality, SEO requires ongoing optimization and adhering to ethical practices to ensure long-term success.

In conclusion, SEO plays a critical role in the digital landscape, and businesses must optimize their websites to rank higher in search results. In the following chapters, we will delve deeper into the various aspects of SEO, such as keyword research, on-page optimization, and backlinking, to help you achieve SEO success.

CHAPTER 2: KEYWORD RESEARCH

In this digital age, it is becoming increasingly difficult for businesses to reach their target audience. The primary reason is that consumers use search engines to find what they are looking for. Hence, Search Engine Optimization (SEO) is an essential practice to ensure businesses can compete and be visible in their respective online markets.

SEO is the process of optimizing your website to rank higher in search engine results pages (SERPs), with the aim of driving relevant traffic to your website that could result in leads and conversions. The primary goal of SEO is to attract users and provide them with a good user experience while they are on your website. While it's important to understand the basics of SEO, it's crucial to note that keyword research is the foundation of any successful SEO strategy.

What are keywords and why are they important?

A keyword is a word or phrase used by consumers to find information through search engines. Keyword research is the process of identifying the search terms and phrases consumers use when looking for specific products or services. In other words, it is about understanding and targeting the phrases your customers use to search for the particular products or services you offer.

Keyword research is an important aspect of SEO as it helps businesses understand their target market better. The insights gained from keyword research allow businesses to understand the language used by their customers when searching for their products or services. This in turn helps businesses to create content that satisfies the searcher's intent and increases the likelihood of ranking higher in search engine results.

Keyword research tools

Gone are the days where businesses had to guess what their customers were searching for online. There are several keyword research tools available in the market today that make it easier to find and analyze the search terms consumers use to find specific products or services. Some of the popular keyword research tools include Google Keyword Planner, Ahrefs, and SEMrush.

Google Keyword Planner is a free keyword research tool that helps businesses discover new keywords and provides insights on existing keywords. The tool also provides data on search volume, competition, and suggested bid amounts for each keyword. Apart from finding relevant keywords, businesses can also use data insights from this tool to adjust their targeting and capture more relevant traffic.

Ahrefs and SEMrush are paid keyword research tools that provide comprehensive insights into keyword data. These tools provide valuable information such as keyword difficulty (how hard it is to rank for a particular keyword), competitor's keywords, backlink data, and more.

How to choose the right keywords

Choosing the right keywords is an important aspect of any SEO strategy, and it requires an understanding of both the business and consumer behaviours. The process of selecting keywords should start with identifying and understanding the business and its offering. Businesses should gain insights into what sets their products or services apart from their competitors. Once the business understands this, they can create a list of keywords and begin to evaluate them using consumer data, search volume, and competition.

When choosing the right keyword, it's important to consider some specific factors that can influence the potential for success, such as search volume, competition level, relevance and intent. Businesses need to avoid choosing broad keywords, which are highly competitive, and instead choose long-tail keywords that are more specific to their products and services.

Long-tail vs. short-tail keywords

Long-tail keywords are longer phrases that describe your product or service in greater detail. They typically have less search volume, are more specific, and have lower competition. Because of these factors, long-tail keywords often lead to higher quality traffic and a better conversion rate.

Conversely, short-tail keywords are short phrases that describe your product or service, but in less detail. They have higher search volume, are less specific, and have higher competition. While short-tail keywords can drive more traffic, it doesn't necessarily mean that the traffic will convert into customers.

Competitive analysis

Competitor analysis is a critical part of a keyword research strategy. Understanding the keywords that competitors are using to drive traffic helps businesses identify opportunities in the market. Through competitive analysis, businesses can learn what their competitors are ranking for and find ways to outrank them.

Keyword mapping

Keyword mapping is the process of assigning keywords to specific pages on your website. It's an important practice that helps ensure that each page on your website is optimized for specific keywords, making it easier to rank higher in search engine results.

Keyword optimization

Once you have identified the keywords you want to target, it's important to incorporate them into your website. This is called keyword optimization, which involves including targeted keywords in specific places, such as title tags, meta descriptions, header tags, and content.

Keyword stuffing and over-optimization

While incorporating keywords is important, businesses should avoid the practice of keyword stuffing which is the act of repeatedly using the same keywords throughout the content. Not only does it provide a poor user experience, but it can also lead to penalties by search engines. Over-optimization is also an issue. Keyword optimization should not compromise the natural flow of the content. striking the right balance is critical to achieving results.

In conclusion, keyword research is a fundamental aspect of SEO and requires an in-depth understanding of the target market, consumer behavior, and the products or services offered by the business. By performing thorough keyword research, businesses can better understand the language their customers are speaking, create targeted content, and generate higher quality traffic to the website. The key to successful SEO is to choose the right keywords, incorporate them into the website's structure, and maintain a natural keyword density that provides the best possible user experience.

CHAPTER 3: ON-PAGE OPTIMIZATION

On-page optimization is the process of optimizing individual pages on your website to improve their search engine ranking and drive more traffic to your site. This involves optimizing various elements on the page, from the content itself to the code that underlies it. In this chapter, we'll cover some of the most important on-page optimization strategies you can use to improve your SEO.

Title Tags and Meta Descriptions

Title tags and meta descriptions are two of the most important on-page optimization elements. These are the snippets of text that appear in search engine results pages (SERPs) when your page is listed.

The title tag is the text that appears at the top of the browser window or tab. It should be descriptive and accurately reflect the content of the page, while also including one or more keywords.

The meta description is a short paragraph that appears below the title tag in search results. It should be compelling and informative, encouraging users to click through to your site. While meta descriptions don't directly affect your search rankings, they can help improve click-through rates, which can have a positive effect on your rankings over time.

Header Tags and Content Optimization

Header tags (H1, H2, H3, etc.) are used to structure content on your page and make it easier for both users and search engines to understand. H1 tags should typically be used for the page title, while H2, H3, and other header tags can be used for subheadings and supporting content.

Your content itself should also be optimized with relevant keywords without being over-optimizing. This means include the keyword in a natural way where it fits within the content without sounding forced.

URL Structure and Permalinks

URLs should be short, simple, and descriptive, containing keywords where appropriate. This enhances the chances of your site ranking high in search engine results and will also make it easier for users to remember your URL and share it with others.

Permalinks are the permanent URLs that link to your individual posts, pages, and other content. They should be optimized with descriptive language and relevant keywords. Avoid using numbers or other characters that don't make sense to readers, and make sure your URLs are unique for each page.

Image Optimization

Images are an important part of many websites, and they should be optimized for both users and search engines. This includes using descriptive filenames, alt tags and optimizing file sizes.

Images can often slow down page load times, so it's important to compress them where necessary to minimize the time it takes for your page to load.

Internal Linking

Internal linking means linking to other pages on your website from within the content on a given page. This helps users navigate your site and also helps search engines better understand the structure and hierarchy of your site.

Internal links should be natural and flow easily, allowing users to navigate from one page to another easily. Avoid over-optimizing internal links and using the same anchor text repeatedly.

Schema Markup

Schema markup is a code that identifies important information on your website, such as business hours, reviews, contact information, and more. This can help increase the chances of your site being featured in rich snippets in search results.

Mobile Optimization

Mobile optimization refers to the practice of ensuring that your website is optimized for viewing on mobile devices. This means that it should be easy to navigate, load quickly, and be responsive to different screen sizes. With a majority of search queries coming from mobile devices, optimizing for mobile is a crucial factor for improving your SEO.

Page Speed and Site Performance

Page speed and site performance are critical for providing a good user experience and improving SEO. Pages that load slowly or are poorly optimized can discourage users from staying on your site or returning in the future.

To improve your page speed and site performance, start by minimizing file sizes, optimizing your code and decreasing HTTP requests. You should also consider using a content delivery network (CDN) to help improve the loading times of your pages.

In conclusion, on-page optimization is a crucial factor in improving your SEO and driving more traffic to your website. By optimizing these key elements on each page, you can help search engines better understand your content and improve the user experience for your visitors. By optimizing page speed and site performance, you can ensure that your site is fully optimized for both users and search engines, thereby enhancing your growth and business success.

CHAPTER 4: CONTENT CREATION

In the world of SEO, content creation is the backbone of every successful strategy. Without high-quality, relevant, and engaging content, your website will struggle to rank in search engine results pages (SERPs). In this chapter, we will explore the importance of content creation, the different types of content, content planning and strategy, optimization and distribution, user-generated content, content promotion, and measuring content performance.

Importance of High-Quality Content

One of the primary goals of SEO is to provide value to users by offering the best possible answers to their search queries. The best way to achieve this is through high-quality content that informs, educates, entertains, or solves users' problems. Search engines prioritize sites that offer superior content, as it drives traffic, increases engagement, and encourages other websites to link back to your pages.

Types of Content

There are many different types of content that you can create, including blog posts, articles, infographics, videos, podcasts, whitepapers, case studies, e-books, webinars, and more. Each has its unique strengths and formats, and it is important to choose the right types of content for your audience and marketing goals.

For example, if you are targeting visual learners, infographics and videos may be more effective than text-based content. If you are trying to showcase your thought leadership in a particular industry, whitepapers and webinars may be more appropriate.

Content Planning and Strategy

Before you start creating content, it is crucial to have a plan and a strategy in place. A content plan outlines the topics, formats, and frequency of content that you will produce. It should align with your audience's interests, needs, and pain points, as well as your business objectives. A content strategy encompasses the tactics, resources, and channels that you will use to create, distribute, and promote your content. It should consider your target audience, your competitive landscape, and your available budget and resources.

Content Optimization

Creating high-quality content is just the first step. You also need to optimize your content for search engines and users. This includes using keywords strategically, organizing your content with headings and subheadings, optimizing your images with descriptive alt tags and filenames, and ensuring that your content is easy to read and digest. It is also critical to ensure that your content is original, relevant, and valuable to your audience.

Content Distribution

Once you have created and optimized your content, you need to distribute it through various channels to reach your target audience. This includes publishing it on your website, sharing it through social media, email marketing, and industry forums, and collaborating with influencers and other websites to gain exposure. You can also syndicate your content on other platforms, such as Medium, LinkedIn, or guest blogging sites, to reach new audiences and earn backlinks.

User-Generated Content

User-generated content (UGC) refers to any content that is created by your audience, such as reviews, comments, social media posts, or testimonials. UGC can enhance your SEO efforts by providing fresh, authentic, and relevant content that is valuable to your audience. It can also increase user engagement, social proof, and loyalty, as well as foster a sense of community and connection with your brand.

Content Promotion

Creating great content is only half the battle; promoting it effectively is the other half. You need to use various tactics and channels to get your content in front of your audience. This can include social media advertising, influencer marketing, email marketing, paid search, and remarketing. It is crucial to track and measure the effectiveness of your content promotion efforts to identify what works best and adjust your strategy accordingly.

Measuring Content Performance

Finally, to determine the success of your content efforts, you need to track and measure key metrics, such as traffic, engagement, conversions, and backlinks. You can use various tools, such as Google Analytics, SEMRush, or Ahrefs, to monitor your content performance and improve your strategy over time. It is important to remember that content creation is an ongoing process that requires constant testing, tweaking, and improvement to achieve optimal SEO results.

In conclusion, content creation is a crucial component of any successful SEO strategy. By creating high-quality, relevant, and engaging content that resonates with your audience, you can increase your website's visibility, traffic, and conversions. However, content creation is not a one-time event but an ongoing process that requires planning, optimization, distribution, promotion, and measurement. By following best practices and continuously improving your content strategy, you can achieve your SEO goals and stand out in a crowded digital landscape.

CHAPTER 5:
BACKLINKS

As you get into the nitty-gritty of SEO, it becomes apparent that backlinks are one of the most important aspects of ranking higher on search engines. A backlink is when one website links to another website. The more backlinks a site has, the higher the site is likely to rank on Google.

In this chapter, we will cover what backlinks are, why they are so important, and how you can acquire quality backlinks to improve your search rankings.

What are backlinks?

Backlinks are links that point towards your website from another website. Search engines look at the backlinks pointing to your site as a "vote" or recommendation for your content, indicating that your site has valuable content worth sharing. The more quality links your site has, the more likely it is to be deemed authoritative.

Why are backlinks important?

Backlinks are important for several reasons:

❖ Authority: Search engines look at the number and quality of backlinks as a vote of confidence in your website. The more authoritative the site linking to you, the more authority it passes on to your site.

❖ Traffic: Backlinks from a high-traffic website can drive referral traffic to your site, which in turn can lead to higher conversions and revenue.

❖ Indexing: Backlinks are one of the primary ways search engines discover new web pages, helping to ensure that your site is indexed and accessible for searchers.

❖ Trust: Links from authoritative sources can help build trust with search engines and visitors, making it more likely that they will return and recommend your site to others.

How to acquire quality backlinks

Now that you understand why backlinks are so essential, let's explore effective strategies for acquiring quality backlinks.

1. Publish high-quality content

The first step in acquiring backlinks is to have high-quality and engaging content on your site. If your content is not valuable or interesting, other sites are unlikely to link to you. Start by creating high-quality blog posts, guides, e-books, infographics, and other resources that your audience will find valuable, then promote that content to earn backlinks.

2. Guest blogging

Guest blogging is the practice of writing content as a guest author on a relevant blog or website, including a link back to your own website. Look for opportunities to contribute guest posts to authoritative websites in your niche, building relationships with those sites' editors and content creators, and including relevant and valuable links back to your site.

3. Broken link building

Broken link building involves finding broken links on other websites in your niche and offering to replace them with a link to your own content. Find relevant websites with broken links using link analysis tools and offer to replace them with a relevant link to your content.

4. Skyscraper technique

The Skyscraper technique is a tactic for creating high-quality content that is better than what is currently available on the web and then reaching out to other websites to encourage backlinks to it. Start by identifying highly-ranked content in your niche, create something better, then reach out to websites that linked to the original content to let them know about your superior alternative.

5. Link reclamation

Link reclamation is the process of finding broken or uncredited backlinks to your site, and reaching out to the websites that posted those links to ask them to fix them. Tools like Google Webmaster Tools can help you identify these opportunities to reclaim lost links.

6. Avoiding link spam

Avoiding link spam is essential; most search engines can detect and penalize any sites that participate in "black hat" backlinking techniques like link farms, comment spam, or paid link building services. Instead, focus on creating high-quality content and earning links naturally.

Conclusion

Backlinks are a critical aspect of SEO. By obtaining quality backlinks to your site from authoritative websites, you can improve your search engine rankings, drive more traffic to your site, and build trust with your audience and with search engines.

By following the strategies outlined in this chapter, you can acquire quality backlinks and increase your website's authority, visibility, and traffic. Remember, building backlinks is not the only component of an effective SEO strategy, but is an important one that should not be ignored.

CHAPTER 6:
TECHNICAL SEO

You've got your keyword research done, you've optimized your content, and you've built some quality backlinks. So, why aren't you ranking higher in Google?

Well, it might be time to take a closer look at the technical side of things. Technical SEO refers to the behind-the-scenes work that affects search engine crawling and indexing. Here's what you need to know:

Website architecture

The way your website is structured can impact how easy it is for search engines to crawl and index your pages. Ideally, your site should have a clear hierarchy, with a home page that links to your main category pages, which then link to your individual product or service pages. This makes it easy for search engines to understand the relationship between your pages.

If your site is disorganized or has a lot of pages buried deep within the site, it can be difficult for search engines to find and index all of your content. Consider creating a sitemap to help guide search engines to your most important pages.

Sitemap creation and submission

A sitemap is a file that lists all the pages on your website and provides information about each page, such as when it was last updated. Search engines use sitemaps to understand the structure of your site and to locate new pages. You can create a sitemap manually or use a tool to generate one automatically.

Once you have a sitemap, you need to submit it to Google and other search engines. This ensures that they can easily find and index all of your pages.

Robots.txt files

A robots.txt file is a text file that tells search engines which pages or sections of your website they should not crawl and index. This can be useful if you have pages that you don't want to appear in search results, such as login pages or admin pages.

However, if you use a robots.txt file incorrectly, you can accidentally block search engines from indexing important pages on your site. Be sure to double-check your robots.txt file to make sure you're not blocking anything you want to appear in search results.

Canonicalization

Canonicalization refers to the process of choosing a preferred URL for a given page. For example, if you have two pages with similar content, you might want to choose one as the "canonical" version and redirect the other page to it.

This can help prevent duplicate content issues, which can hurt your search engine rankings. Make sure to set up canonical tags correctly on your pages to tell search engines which version of a page is the one you want them to index.

HTTPS and SSL certificates

Google has been urging website owners to switch to HTTPS (secure hypertext transfer protocol) for several years now. HTTPS is a more secure version of the standard http protocol, which is used to transmit data between a website and its users.

By using HTTPS, you add an extra layer of security to your website, which can help protect user data and build trust with visitors. In addition, Google has indicated that HTTPS is a ranking factor, meaning using it could help your site rank higher in search results.

To use HTTPS, you'll need to purchase an SSL (secure sockets layer) certificate and install it on your website. This can be done through your web hosting provider or through a third-party provider.

Duplicate content issues

As mentioned earlier, having duplicate content on your website can hurt your search engine rankings. Duplicate content can arise from several different scenarios, such as having identical pages on different domains or having multiple versions of a page with slightly different URLs.

To avoid duplicate content issues, make sure each page on your site has a unique URL and content. If you have pages with similar content, use canonical tags or redirects to point search engines to the preferred version.

Redirects

Sometimes you may need to redirect users from one page to another, such as when you delete a page or change its URL. There are several types of redirects you can use, but the most common are 301 redirects and 302 redirects.

A 301 redirect is a permanent redirect that tells search engines that the content has moved permanently to a new URL. This passes on the link juice (ranking power) of the old page to the new one, which can help preserve your search engine rankings.

A 302 redirect, on the other hand, is a temporary redirect that indicates the content has only moved temporarily. This does not pass on link juice, meaning it can hurt your search engine rankings if used on a permanent basis.

Site migration

If you're planning to move your website to a new domain or hosting provider, it's important to handle the migration carefully to avoid losing search engine rankings. Site migrations can be complex, but some important steps to take include:

- Informing search engines of the move with a 301 redirect
- Updating your sitemap and robots.txt files
- Checking for broken links and fixing them
- Updating any external links pointing to your site
- Monitoring your search engine rankings after the move

By taking these steps, you can help ensure a smooth transition and minimize any potentially negative impacts on your search engine rankings.

In conclusion, technical SEO is an important part of any comprehensive SEO strategy. By optimizing your website structure, using canonical tags, handling redirects carefully, and taking other technical steps, you can help improve your search engine rankings and drive more traffic to your website.

CHAPTER 7:
LOCAL SEO

Search engine optimization (SEO) is an important aspect of any digital marketing strategy. It is a series of techniques aimed at improving visibility on search engines like Google and Bing. In recent times, local SEO has become increasingly important. Local SEO is a way to optimize your website in a way that it appears higher on search engine results pages for specific areas, cities, or regions. In this chapter, we will discuss the basics of local SEO, how to measure its performance, and the various tools that can be used for local SEO optimization.

What is Local SEO?

Local SEO is the process of optimizing your website for local search queries. It involves making your website relevant to a specific geographic area, such as a city, state, or region. Local SEO has become increasingly important due to the rise of mobile devices and the need for mobile users to find businesses quickly and easily. Local search results include maps, contact information, reviews, and ratings. Local SEO not only helps businesses reach consumers in their local area but also helps them rank higher in search results.

Google My Business Optimization

One of the most important factors in local SEO is Google My Business. Google My Business is a free tool offered by Google that allows businesses to create a profile that shows up when someone searches for them on Google or Google Maps. It includes important information such as the business's hours, location, phone number, website, and more. When optimizing your Google My Business profile, it's important to ensure that your business information is accurate and up-to-date. This includes adding photos and videos, responding to reviews, and optimizing your business category.

Local Keyword Research

Keyword research is a critical component of local SEO. It's important to identify the keywords and phrases that customers are using to find your business. The SERP analysis will show you which keywords your competitors are using, and the Google Keyword Planner can help you identify relevant keywords, and ad campaigns. When conducting keyword research for local SEO, it's also important to consider "near me" searches and "location" searches to ensure this query is included in your keywords.

Local Citation Building

Another important aspect of local SEO is citation building. Citations are online mentions of your business that include the business's name, address, and phone number (NAP). Local citation building involves adding your business to online directories, local business directories, and niche directories such as Yelp, TripAdvisor, and Angie's List. It's important that your NAP information is consistent across all directories.

NAP Consistency

Ensuring that your NAP information is consistent on all directories is crucial. Google checks the consistency of this information across all directories and looks for any discrepancies in your contact information that could impact your business's result rankings. Make sure to list your business name, address, and phone number as they appear on your website on all external directories.

Location-based Content

Adding location-based content is an effective way to optimize your website for local SEO. Location-based content can include references to the city, town, or region where your business is located. This content can be in the form of blog posts, articles, or pages. Location-based content can also include photographs and videos of your business in a specific location, client testimonials, or supporting information about nearby businesses.

Online Reviews and Reputation Management

Online reviews play a crucial role in local SEO. Positive reviews can help your business rank higher in search engine results pages. Google My Business tool allows business owners to manage the reviews left on their profile. It's important to monitor and respond to reviews to provide excellent customer service and build a positive online reputation. Reputation management is critical in building strong consumer relations.

Local Link Building

Link building is an essential aspect of SEO. Local link building is the practice of earning backlinks from other businesses in your industry or niche that operate in the same locality. Attending networking events or location-specific meetups could allow for higher chance of earning links. Make sure your information in these actions points back to your website in order to benefit SEO.

Conclusion

Local SEO is an essential component of any digital marketing strategy for businesses that operate in a specific locality. Optimizing your Google My Business profile, conducting local keyword research, building consistent NAP citations, implementing location-based content, and monitoring online reviews and ratings are essential in achieving higher rankings in search engine results pages. Local SEO optimization requires a concerted effort with continued monitoring to experience desired results.

CHAPTER 8: E-COMMERCE SEO

E-commerce SEO is a unique field because it has its own set of challenges and opportunities. Unlike traditional websites, e-commerce sites have numerous product pages, each with its own set of variables, such as size, color, and price. This means that the optimization process must take into account these variables, as well as the different stages of the purchasing process.

Unique challenges of e-commerce SEO

One of the biggest challenges of e-commerce SEO is the size of the site. Large e-commerce sites can have thousands of product pages, which can make it difficult to optimize each page individually. This is why it's important to have a clear site structure and make the most important pages easily accessible to both users and search engines.

Another challenge is the difficulty of creating unique product descriptions. Many e-commerce sites use manufacturer descriptions, which can be duplicated across multiple sites, resulting in duplicate content issues. To avoid this, e-commerce sites must create unique product descriptions that highlight the features and benefits of each product.

Product descriptions and optimization

Product descriptions are a critical part of e-commerce SEO

because they provide valuable information to customers and search engines. Search engines use product descriptions to determine the relevance of a page to a specific keyword. This means that product descriptions should be optimized with relevant keywords to help them rank higher in search results.

Optimizing product descriptions involves using the right keywords, optimizing the content for both users and search engines, and including product details such as size, color, and price. It's important to avoid keyword stuffing, as this can result in penalties and negatively impact the user experience.

Category pages and site architecture

Category pages are important for e-commerce sites because they help customers navigate through the site and find the products they are looking for. From an SEO perspective, category pages provide an opportunity to target specific keywords and improve the overall site structure.

Category pages should be optimized with relevant keywords and provide clear descriptions of the products that fall under that category. It's important to structure the site in a way that makes it easy for customers and search engines to navigate. This means having a clear hierarchy of pages, using breadcrumb navigation, and linking to related products and categories.

Faceted navigation

Faceted navigation is a feature commonly used in e-commerce sites to help customers filter and sort products based on different attributes, such as size, color, and price. While faceted navigation can be helpful for customers, it can also create duplicate content issues and make it difficult for search engines to crawl the site.

To avoid duplicate content issues, it's important to use canonical tags to indicate the preferred version of the page and avoid indexing pages with too many filters applied. It's also important to include a nofollow tag on internal search pages to prevent search engines from crawling them.

Duplicate content issues

Duplicate content is a common issue in e-commerce SEO due to the use of manufacturer descriptions and the presence of variations of the same product. Duplicate content can negatively impact the user experience and make it difficult for search engines to determine the relevance of a page to a specific keyword.

To avoid duplicate content issues, e-commerce sites should create unique product descriptions, use canonical tags to indicate the preferred version of a page, and use the rel=alternate tag to indicate alternate versions of a page.

Reviews and ratings

Customer reviews and ratings are an important part of e-commerce SEO because they provide valuable information to both customers and search engines. Search engines use reviews and ratings to determine the relevance and authority of a page, and customers consider them when making purchasing decisions.

To optimize customer reviews and ratings, it's important to encourage customers to leave feedback, monitor and respond to reviews, and incorporate them into the site structure, such as including them on product pages and category pages.

Cart abandonment

Cart abandonment is a common issue in e-commerce, and it can negatively impact both the user experience and the SEO performance of the site. Cart abandonment occurs when a customer adds a product to their cart but doesn't complete the checkout process.

To reduce cart abandonment, e-commerce sites should provide a clear and simple checkout process, offer multiple payment options, and include security badges to build trust with customers. It's also important to have a retargeting strategy in place to bring customers back to the site and complete their purchase.

International SEO considerations

International SEO is an important consideration for e-commerce sites that sell products in multiple countries. International SEO requires a different approach than traditional SEO because it involves considerations such as language and currency.

To optimize for international SEO, e-commerce sites should use language-specific URLs, translate, and optimize content for each language, and include currency and pricing information for each country. It's also important to comply with legal and regulatory requirements for each country and use hreflang tags to indicate the language and country targeting of each page.

In conclusion, e-commerce SEO has its own unique set of challenges and opportunities. Optimizing product descriptions, category pages, and site structure are critical for improving the SEO performance of an e-commerce site. Managing faceted navigation, avoiding duplicate content, and optimizing reviews and ratings are also important considerations. Finally, e-commerce sites that sell products in multiple countries must implement an effective international SEO strategy to reach their global audience.

CHAPTER 9: ANALYTICS AND MEASUREMENT

In the world of SEO, there is no such thing as "set it and forget it." One of the most important aspects of any SEO campaign is tracking and measurement. Without proper tracking and measurement, it's impossible to know if your efforts are paying off or if you need to pivot your strategy. In this chapter, we'll dive deep into the world of SEO analytics and measurement to help you understand how to track, measure, and communicate SEO results effectively.

The Importance of Tracking and Measurement

Before we dive into the specifics of tracking and measurement, let's talk about why it's so important. The ultimate goal of SEO is to drive more traffic to your website and ultimately convert that traffic into customers. However, you can't improve what you don't measure. By tracking and measuring your SEO efforts, you'll be able to identify what's working, what's not working, and make data-driven decisions to improve your results.

Another important aspect of tracking and measurement is accountability. If you're working with an SEO agency or managing an in-house SEO team, it's crucial to have clear performance metrics in place to ensure everyone is working towards the same goals. By tracking and measuring your SEO performance, you'll be able to identify areas where your team is excelling and areas where improvement is needed.

Google Analytics Setup and Implementation

The first step in tracking and measuring your SEO efforts is to set up Google Analytics. Google Analytics is a free tool that provides valuable insights into your website traffic, including how visitors are finding your site, what pages they are visiting, and how long they are staying on your site.

To get started with Google Analytics, you'll need to create an account and add the tracking code to your website. This code will track visitor behavior on your site and send data back to Google Analytics.

Once you have Google Analytics set up, you can start tracking and measuring your SEO performance using a variety of metrics, including:

- ❖ Organic search traffic: This metric measures how many visitors are coming to your site from organic search results.

- ❖ Bounce rate: This metric tracks the percentage of visitors who leave your site after only viewing one page.

- ❖ Pages per session: This metric measures how many pages visitors view on average during a session on your site.

- ❖ Average session duration: This metric measures how long visitors are staying on your site during a single session.

- ❖ Conversion rate: This metric tracks the percentage of visitors who take a desired action on your site, such as making a purchase or filling out a contact form.

Key Metrics to Track

While the metrics listed above are important, there are several other key metrics you should track to measure the success of your SEO efforts. These include:

❖ Keyword rankings: Tracking your keyword rankings helps you understand how your site is performing in search engine results pages (SERPs). You should track your rankings for your target keywords on a regular basis to identify trends and opportunities for optimization.

❖ Backlink profile: Your backlink profile is an important factor in SEO. Tracking the number and quality of your backlinks can help you identify areas where you need to improve your link building efforts.

❖ Click-through rate (CTR): CTR measures the percentage of users who click on your website listing in search results. Improving your CTR can lead to more traffic and higher rankings.

❖ Time on page: This metric measures how long visitors spend on a specific page on your site. Pages with longer average times on page can indicate that visitors are finding the content valuable and engaging.

❖ Exit rate: Exit rate measures the percentage of visitors who leave your site from a specific page. High exit rates on certain pages may indicate issues with site usability or content quality.

A/B Testing and Experimentation

Another important aspect of measuring SEO performance is A/B testing and experimentation. A/B testing involves testing two different versions of a page to see which one performs better in terms of traffic, engagement, and conversions.

By running A/B tests, you can identify which elements of your site are performing well and which ones need improvement. For example, you can test different headlines or calls-to-action to see which ones drive more conversions.

Conversion Rate Optimization

Speaking of conversions, conversion rate optimization (CRO) is another important aspect of measuring SEO success. CRO is the process of optimizing your website to encourage more visitors to take a desired action, such as filling out a contact form or making a purchase.

CRO involves testing different designs, copy, and layouts to determine which ones lead to the highest conversion rates. By improving your conversion rate, you'll be able to generate more leads and revenue from your existing traffic.

Attribution Modeling

Another metric to consider when measuring SEO performance is attribution modeling. Attribution modeling is the process of determining which marketing channels are driving the most conversions on your website.

There are several different types of attribution models, including first touch, last touch, and multi-touch. Each model assigns credit to different touchpoints in the customer journey, helping you understand which channels are most effective at driving conversions.

Tools for Tracking SEO Performance

There are several tools available to help you track and measure your SEO performance. Some of these tools include:

- ❖ Google Search Console: Google Search Console provides valuable insights into your site's performance in Google search results, including keyword rankings and click-through rates.

❖ SEMrush: SEMrush is a popular SEO tool that provides keyword research, backlink analysis, and competitor research.

❖ Ahrefs: Ahrefs is another popular SEO tool that provides backlink analysis, keyword research, and competitor analysis.

❖ Moz: Moz is an all-in-one SEO tool that includes keyword research, link building, and site audit features.

❖ Google Analytics: As mentioned earlier, Google Analytics is a free tool that provides insights into your website traffic, visitor behavior, and conversion rates.

Reporting and Communicating Results

Once you have tracked and measured your SEO performance, it's important to report and communicate your results effectively. This involves identifying the key metrics that matter to your stakeholders and presenting them in a clear and concise manner.

When reporting SEO results, it's important to focus on trends rather than individual data points. For example, instead of reporting on the number of visitors to your site in a specific month, focus on the trend over time. Are your visitor numbers increasing, decreasing, or staying the same?

When communicating SEO results, it's also important to tie your efforts back to business goals. For example, if your goal is to increase leads, report on how many leads your SEO efforts have generated rather than just reporting on traffic numbers.

Conclusion

Tracking and measuring SEO performance is crucial to the success of any SEO campaign. By setting up Google Analytics, tracking key metrics, experimenting with A/B testing, optimizing for conversions, and communicating results effectively, you'll be able to make data-driven decisions that drive more traffic, engagement, and revenue to your website.

CHAPTER 10:
SEO TOOLS AND RESOURCES

SEO is a vast field that entails a lot of different aspects, from research to implementation. As a result, there are several tools and resources available to SEO professionals to help them achieve their objectives. These tools help maximize productivity, automate repetitive tasks, and facilitate analysis. Before discussing these tools in greater detail, it's important to remember that tools are not the be-all and end-all of SEO. They must be supplemented with a thorough understanding of SEO principles and an overarching strategy.

Keyword Research Tools

Keyword research is a fundamental aspect of SEO, and there are many tools available to help you with it. Here are some of the most popular ones:

❖ Google Keyword Planner: This tool is free and provides you with keyword ideas, search volume data, and cost-per-click (CPC) estimates. Google Keyword Planner can also help you discover new keywords by looking at what visitors search for on Google.

❖ Ahrefs: A comprehensive SEO tool, Ahrefs provides various keyword research tools, including a keyword explorer tool and a content explorer tool. These tools can help you generate long-tail keyword ideas and assist with competitive analysis.

❖ SEMrush: Another all-encompassing SEO tool, SEMrush provides keyword suggestion tools that offer information on keyword difficulty, search volume, and related keywords. You can also use SEMrush to perform competitive research and gain insight into which keywords your competitors are ranking for.

❖ Moz: Moz provides a straightforward keyword research tool that allows you to find keywords relevant to your business by entering a phrase or term that describes your business. Moz's keyword explorer tool also provides information on keyword volume, difficulty, and organic click-through rate (CTR).

On-Page Optimization Tools

On-page optimization is one of the most crucial aspects of SEO. Here are some tools that can help you with on-page optimization:

❖ Yoast SEO: A plugin for WordPress, Yoast SEO provides a checklist of tasks that need to be addressed on a page-by-page basis for optimal on-page optimization. These tasks involve optimizing the meta title and description, ensuring the presence of a keyword in the content, and other technical aspects of optimization.

❖ Google Analytics: While Google Analytics isn't typically thought of as an on-page optimization tool, it can nevertheless help identify areas of improvement. For example, tracking metrics like bounce rate and time on page can help you understand how visitors interact with your website, giving you a better idea of how to optimize pages for better performance.

❖   SEMrush: Semrush also has an on-page SEO tool that analyzes the elements of a webpage and suggests improvements for particular pages. The SEMrush on-page SEO tool provides suggestions for meta tags and other structural elements, alongside guidelines for making content more readable.

Backlink Analysis Tools

Backlinks are important for SEO because they signal to search engines that a particular website has authoritative content. Here are some of the best backlink analysis tools available:

❖   Ahrefs: One of the most powerful backlink analysis tools, Ahrefs provides detailed information on backlinks to a website. The tool can evaluate the quantity and quality of links, as well as provide insight into the anchor text, and overall domain authority of the sites linking back to you.

❖   Majestic: Majestic provides link metrics that can help you evaluate the authority and relevance of links pointing to your website. Its TrustFlow and CitationFlow metrics are especially useful for identifying high-quality links.

❖   SEMrush: SEMrush's backlink checking tool can be used to identify new and lost backlinks, as well as competitor backlinks. You can also use SEMrush to analyze anchor text and backlink metrics.

Technical SEO Tools

Technical SEO involves optimizing the technical aspects of a website, including URL structure, site speed, and schema markup. Here are some of the best technical SEO tools available:

❖   Google Search Console: Google Search Console provides insight into various aspects of site performance, including crawl errors, mobile-friendliness, and sitemaps. It also allows you to submit sitemaps and requests for re-indexing of content.

❖ SEMrush: SEMrush has an auditing tool that provides a comprehensive analysis of the technical aspects of a website. The tool can analyze site speed, crawlability, and index issues, as well as provide insight into areas of improvement.

Local SEO Tools

Local SEO is crucial for businesses that operate in certain geographic areas. Here are some of the best tools for local SEO:

❖ Google My Business: The Google My Business platform is vital for local businesses, as it provides an opportunity to list contact information and business hours. You can also post images, update your business description, and respond to reviews.

❖ Moz Local: Moz Local is a tool that helps businesses manage their business listings and citations across various platforms. The tool can also help identify opportunities for improvement in citations and link building.

❖ Yext: Yext provides a platform for managing local listings across multiple services and directories, allowing you to quickly update hours, addresses, and other information.

Content Creation and Optimization Tools

Creating and optimizing content is key for SEO success. Here are some of the best tools for doing so:

❖ BuzzSumo: BuzzSumo allows you to identify popular topics and content that is currently performing well in your industry. You can use this information to create better content that resonates with your audience.

❖ Grammarly: Grammarly is an essential tool for ensuring that content is high-quality and free from errors. Its basic version is free, while premium versions offer more advanced features.

❖ Hootsuite: Hootsuite is a social media management tool that allows you to optimize your content by scheduling posts at optimal times and monitoring performance across multiple platforms.

Analytics and Reporting Tools

Tracking and measuring SEO performance is essential for understanding the impact of your strategies. Here are some tools that can help:

❖ Google Analytics: A versatile and powerful tool, Google Analytics provides insight into various aspects of website performance. You can use it to track traffic sources, user behavior, and conversions.

❖ SEMrush: SEMrush provides a suite of tools for analyzing and reporting on SEO performance. Its dashboard allows you to track keyword rankings, backlinks, and competitor analysis, among other things.

❖ Reporting frameworks: Several frameworks exist for reporting on SEO performance, including the Google Data Studio, which allows you to create customizable dashboards and reports using data from multiple sources.

SEO is a complex field that requires a lot of dedication, effort, and knowledge to achieve success. Fortunately, there are many tools and resources available that can help make the process easier. By taking advantage of these tools, SEO professionals can maximize their productivity and stay ahead of the competition. However, it's important to remember that these tools are merely supplements to an overarching SEO strategy, and that a thorough understanding of SEO best practices is crucial for success.

CHAPTER 11: SEO AND SOCIAL MEDIA

Social media platforms are changing the way we communicate with one another. With more than 3 billion people using social media around the world, there has been significant growth in businesses leveraging social media for marketing purposes. In recent years, the effect of social media on organic search results has also been an important factor in search engine optimization (SEO). In this chapter, we'll discuss the relationship between SEO and social media, best practices for making the most of social media for your SEO strategy, and common pitfalls to avoid.

Relationship between SEO and Social Media

The relationship between social media and SEO is not always direct. Search engines like Google claim that they don't use social media metrics, such as likes, shares, and followers, as ranking factors. However, there is evidence that social media can have indirect effects on website traffic, brand awareness, and other factors that can impact SEO. Here are a few ways social media can impact SEO:

❖ Increasing Brand Awareness: When people share or interact with your social media content, it can lead to wider brand exposure and more website traffic. A study by Moz found a correlation between social metrics and search engine rankings, suggesting that search engines may use social engagement as an indicator of brand authority.

❖ Generating High-Quality Backlinks: Social media can be a powerful tool for acquiring quality backlinks to your website. When people share or re-share your content on social media, it can generate links back to your website, indicating to search engines that your content is high-quality, trustworthy, and worth ranking above other similar websites in search engine results.

❖ Increasing Social Signals: Social signals are indications of social media activity related to your website, such as likes, shares, and comments. While not directly a ranking factor, social signals can help to increase the visibility of your website in search engine results. When you share and promote content on social media, it can generate more social signals and increase the authority of your website in search engine results.

Social Media Best Practices for SEO

If you're ready to start using social media to support your SEO strategy, here are a few best practices to keep in mind:

❖ Optimize Your Social Media Profiles: Your social media profiles should be optimized to maximize their potential for SEO. Use the right keywords in your profile descriptions, choose an easy-to-remember username, and use a high-quality profile image. When you optimize your social profiles, they will be more visible in search engine results, and it will be easier for people to find your brand online.

❖ Create High-Quality Social Media Content: Your social media content should be high-quality, shareable, and optimized with relevant keywords. By sharing high-quality content on your social media platforms, you can increase the number of backlinks to your website, driving up your website ranking in search engine results pages.

❖ Promote Your Content on Social Media: Promoting your

content on social media can help to increase engagement and bring more traffic to your website. When you promote your content on social media platforms, you're creating backlink signals that will indicate the authenticity, credibility, and quality of your content to search engines.

❖ Engage with Your Following: Engaging with your followers is an important factor in establishing authenticity and relevance for your brand. By responding to comments, and being active on your social media profiles, you establish trust and interest in your brand, which can lead to more social signals and potentially help your website rank better in search engine results pages.

❖ Use Video Content: Video content is becoming increasingly popular and has a lot of potential for SEO endeavours. By creating high-quality video content and sharing it on social media, you will be able to garner more engagement and generate backlinks. Additionally, videos can help to enhance user experience on your website, which can serve as a ranking signal for search engines.

Social Media Platform Optimization

Different social media platforms have distinct features and requirements when it comes to content optimization, so it's important to tailor your SEO strategy accordingly. Here are a few tips for optimizing your social media profiles on some popular social media networks:

❖ Facebook: Facebook is the largest social media network, with over 2 billion active users. On Facebook, it's important to focus on creating visually compelling content, optimizing post descriptions with relevant keywords, and building a community of followers who share your content.

❖ Twitter: Twitter has over 330 million active users and is known for the speed and frequency of its content.

Optimizing your Twitter profile involves using relevant keywords in your bio and tweets, using relevant hashtags, and engaging with your followers regularly.

❖ Instagram: Instagram is a visual platform with over 1 billion active users. Popular with younger demographics, it is primarily a video and photo sharing platform. Optimizing your Instagram profile involves using relevant keywords in your captions, creating high-quality images and videos, and engaging with followers through likes, comments, and hashtags.

Influencer Marketing

Influencer marketing has become increasingly popular for businesses looking to increase their social media following and create powerful backlinks. Influencers are social media users who have a significant following and are seen as experts or authorities in a particular industry or interest area. When using influencer marketing, it's important to choose influencers who are relevant to your brand, will create quality content, have an engaged following, and have an interest in partnering with your brand.

Social Media Advertising

You can also use social media advertising to drive website traffic and exposure. Social media advertising is making use of the paid promotional tools that are offered by social media platforms, including Facebook ads, Instagram ads, Twitter ads, and LinkedIn ads. This can be effective in promoting your brand to a large and target audience. Be sure to research industry standards, know who you are targeting, and track the results of your social media advertising efforts.

Measuring Success & Avoiding Pitfalls

Any digital marketing efforts, including social media for SEO, should be tracked and measured. Use analytics tools and metrics to track results and determine the effectiveness of your strategy. Some key metrics to track for social media marketing include engagement, reach, impressions, and clicks.

As with any marketing effort, it's important to avoid common pitfalls. One common pitfall is spamming your followers with irrelevant content, which can lead to them disengaging. Also, it's significant to keep an eye out for social media account hacking and negative reviews, minimizing the steps to avoid these can prove to be valuable to your social media marketing.

Conclusion

Social media can be an effective tool for improving SEO, and the interaction between the two channels is expected to continue to grow. By developing a strong social media presence, creating high-quality content, optimizing your social media profiles, and engaging with your followers, you can enhance your SEO strategy and continue to drive website traffic, backlinks, and conversions. While it's a slightly more complex process than click to purchase, social media can maximize the success of an SEO strategy to a remarkable extent.

CHAPTER 12:
MOBILE SEO

With the rise of smartphones and tablets, mobile search has overtaken desktop search. Mobile devices now account for more than 50% of all internet usage worldwide. As a result, mobile optimization has become a crucial aspect of SEO.

Mobile-friendly website design

A mobile-friendly website is designed to display correctly on smaller screens and touch-based devices. Google now prioritizes mobile-friendly sites in its search results. Therefore, it is essential to have a mobile-friendly site to improve your SEO ranking.

Responsive design vs. separate mobile site

There are several ways to make a website mobile-friendly. One is to use responsive design, where your site's layout and content automatically adjust to different screen sizes. Another option is to create a separate mobile site, which is a version of your site specifically designed for mobile devices and linked to your main site. The choice between responsive design and a mobile site depends on your site's design and functionalities. However, responsive design is recommended as it is easier to maintain and ensures that all users get the same content, regardless of the device they're using.

Mobile-specific SEO best practices

Mobile SEO follows the same principles as desktop SEO, but there are some mobile-specific considerations. First, it's important to ensure fast loading times for mobile devices. Mobile users expect sites to load quickly, and Google prioritizes fast-loading sites in its mobile search results.

Second, the usability of your site is also crucial for mobile users. It should be easy to navigate on a smaller screen and have clear calls to action. This includes the ability to tap buttons and links without accidentally clicking on the wrong one.

Third, the layout and design of your site are also essential. It should be easy to read on a mobile device, with large fonts and a clear hierarchy. The menu and content should be easily accessible, and images should be optimized for smaller screens.

Mobile app optimization

In addition to a mobile-friendly website, optimizing your mobile app is also critical for mobile SEO. Mobile apps can appear in Google's mobile search results, but they need to be properly optimized. This includes optimizing the app's title, description, and screenshots for mobile devices. To improve your app's visibility, you can also leverage app store optimization techniques, such as using relevant keywords and getting positive reviews from users.

Mobile search advertising

Mobile search advertising allows businesses to place ads directly in front of mobile users. These ads can appear at the top of mobile search results, above organic results. It's essential to ensure that your search ads are optimized for mobile devices, including having clear calls to action that are easy to tap on a smaller screen.

Voice search optimization

With the rise of smart speakers and virtual assistants like Siri and Google Assistant, voice search has become an important aspect of mobile SEO. Voice searches are often longer and more conversational than text searches, so it's important to optimize your content for natural language queries and incorporate long-tail keywords.

Tracking mobile SEO performance

To track your mobile SEO performance, you should use analytics tools that allow you to monitor mobile traffic and user behavior. Google Analytics provides insights into mobile-specific metrics such as bounce rate, pages per session, and average session duration. It's also important to track your site's mobile loading times and usability with tools like Google's Mobile-Friendly Test and PageSpeed Insights.

Conclusion

Mobile SEO is crucial for any business that wants to improve its online visibility and reach its target audience effectively. By adopting best practices for mobile-friendly website design, mobile-specific SEO strategies, and leveraging the power of mobile apps and search advertising, you can position your business for success in a mobile-first world. Remember to track your mobile SEO performance regularly to ensure you are meeting your goals and objectives and update your strategies accordingly. Optimizing for mobile is an ongoing process, but the benefits of a strong mobile SEO presence are undeniable.

CHAPTER 13: SEO FOR SMALL BUSINESSES

Small businesses face unique challenges when it comes to SEO. Unlike larger organizations, small businesses often have limited resources and smaller budgets to allocate towards marketing efforts. However, this does not mean that small businesses are at a disadvantage in terms of SEO. In fact, local SEO can be a powerful tool for smaller businesses to improve their online visibility and attract new customers.

In this chapter, we will explore the importance of local SEO for small businesses, common mistakes to avoid, and how to build an SEO plan for the long term.

Unique challenges facing small businesses

Small businesses face several unique challenges when it comes to SEO. One of the biggest challenges is the limited resources and budget available for marketing efforts. Often, small business owners wear many hats and may not have a dedicated marketing team or the financial means to outsource SEO. This means that small business owners must be strategic about how they allocate their time and resources towards SEO.

Another challenge is the competition. Small businesses often compete with larger organizations in their industry, making it difficult to stand out in search results. Additionally, small businesses may have limited resources to invest in content creation and link building strategies to improve their rankings.

Importance of local SEO

Despite these challenges, small businesses have a key advantage when it comes to local SEO. Local SEO is focused on improving your online visibility for local search queries. For example, if you run a local bakery, you want to appear in search results when someone in your area searches for "best bakery near me." Local SEO can help your business appear in Google's "Local Pack" and improve your rankings in organic search results.

Local SEO is especially important for small businesses because it allows them to compete with larger organizations on a level playing field. By targeting local keywords, small businesses can improve their rankings in their local area and reach a highly targeted audience.

Balancing SEO with other marketing efforts

When it comes to SEO for small businesses, it's important to balance your efforts with other marketing strategies. SEO is just one piece of the puzzle, and it's important to have a comprehensive marketing plan that includes social media, email marketing, and other channels.

One mistake that small business owners often make is focusing too much on SEO and neglecting other marketing efforts. It's important to allocate your budget and resources towards a variety of marketing channels to reach a wider audience and attract new customers.

DIY vs. outsourcing SEO

Small business owners must decide whether to handle SEO in-house or to outsource to a professional agency. While handling SEO in-house can save money in the short term, it can be time-consuming and may not yield the best results.

Outsourcing SEO to a professional agency can be expensive, but it allows small business owners to focus on other areas of their business while leaving the SEO to the experts. Additionally, professional agencies have the resources and expertise to develop a comprehensive SEO strategy that is tailored to your business's unique needs.

Budgeting for SEO

One of the biggest challenges that small business owners face is budgeting for SEO. SEO can be expensive, and small businesses must be strategic about how they allocate their budget towards marketing efforts.

When budgeting for SEO, it's important to prioritize your efforts. Focus on the areas that will yield the highest return on investment, such as local SEO and content creation. Additionally, it's important to track your progress and adjust your budget accordingly. If certain channels aren't yielding results, it may be time to reallocate your budget towards other channels.

Common mistakes to avoid

Small businesses often make common mistakes when it comes to SEO. One mistake is neglecting local SEO. By targeting local keywords and optimizing your Google My Business listing, you can improve your rankings in your local area and attract more customers.

Another mistake is neglecting content creation. High-quality content is essential for improving your rankings in search results and attracting new customers. Small businesses should focus on creating informative and engaging content that is targeted towards their audience.

Measuring ROI for small businesses

Measuring the return on investment for SEO can be difficult, especially for small businesses that have limited resources to invest in SEO. However, it's important to track your progress and measure the impact of your SEO efforts.

One way to measure the ROI of SEO is to track your website traffic and monitor your keyword rankings. Additionally, you can track your conversions and the source of your incoming traffic. By analyzing this data, you can determine which channels are working and which need to be adjusted.

Building an SEO plan for the long term

When building an SEO plan for your small business, it's important to take a long-term approach. SEO is a marathon, not a sprint, and it takes time to see results.

Start by setting clear goals and objectives for your SEO efforts. This could include improving your rankings for local keywords, increasing your website traffic, or improving your conversion rate. Next, develop a comprehensive SEO strategy that is tailored to your business's unique needs. This should include an analysis of your target audience, keyword research, on-page optimization, content creation, and link building strategies.

Finally, it's important to track your progress and adjust your strategy as needed. SEO is constantly evolving, and it's important to stay up-to-date with industry changes and adjust your strategy accordingly.

Conclusion

SEO is a powerful tool for small businesses to improve their online visibility and attract new customers. While small businesses face unique challenges when it comes to SEO, local SEO can be a powerful way to compete with larger organizations on a level playing field.

By balancing SEO with other marketing efforts, budgeting strategically, and avoiding common mistakes, small businesses can develop a comprehensive SEO plan for the long term and see real results.

CHAPTER 14:
SEO FOR LARGER ORGANIZATIONS

Large organizations have unique challenges when it comes to SEO. These enterprises have multiple websites, coordinate with different departments, ensure that their brands remain consistent, and must measure SEO ROI at scale. In this chapter, we will explore how larger organizations can overcome these challenges and build a thriving SEO strategy.

Dealing with Multiple Websites and Domains:

Large organizations often have several websites for each of its brands and products. While these different websites serve different purposes, they can create confusion for search engines, resulting in poor rankings and wasted SEO efforts. This is where centralized SEO management comes in.

Centralized SEO management refers to having one team or system that handles all SEO activities across all sites and domains. This approach ensures that the brand messaging is consistent, and that the SEO strategy is unified across all channels. Additionally, a centralized approach allows for better resource allocation, streamlines communication, and ensures that optimization opportunities are not missed.

Another approach is to have a network structure with a main

website that links to and promotes other specific websites within the network. This structure helps search engines understand how the different websites within the network are related and enables better SEO results.

Coordinating with Different Departments:

SEO in large organizations requires coordination between different departments like marketing, content creation, web development, IT, and more. Each department brings a unique perspective and expertise that can enhance SEO efforts. However, without proper coordination, these efforts can easily become disjointed.

The key to successful coordination is to have a shared vision across all departments. This means having clear goals and objectives for SEO and making sure that all departments understand how their actions contribute to these goals. Regular communication and collaboration are essential, and each department should know their roles and responsibilities in the overall SEO strategy.

Ensuring Consistency Across Brands:

Large organizations have multiple brands, products, and stakeholders. This could be challenging as messaging and brand identity could vary across the different products creating inconsistent brand value & image.

A centralized SEO management approach can help ensure consistency across brands. This should include brand guidelines, messaging, and visual elements that are adhered to by all departments and stakeholders. This approach helps to establish clear brand standards, ensuring that all messaging, visuals, and content are uniform and aligned with the brand.

Enterprise-level SEO tools and resources:

Larger organizations require enterprise-level tools and resources to manage SEO effectively. Such tools include SEO management platforms, analytics software, link-building tools, and more.

Enterprise-level SEO tools enable organizations to automate SEO tasks, analyze results in greater detail, and manage multiple campaigns through a single interface. It also empowers organizations to integrate SEO with other marketing channels, thus generating better attribution and more growth opportunities.

Measuring SEO ROI at Scale:

Measuring SEO ROI at scale can be challenging for larger organizations due to the variety of products, markets, and stakeholders involved. It is imperative to establish clear SEO goals and metrics for the various campaigns. These metrics should be tracked using an analytics platform to gather data accurately and efficiently.

Evaluating the progress of SEO campaigns at scale requires the integration of data from different sources. Enterprise-level SEO tools or custom dashboards can help with this, enabling organizations to track SEO across different websites, products, and campaigns.

Building an SEO Team and Culture:

Building a strong SEO team and culture is critical for the long-term success of larger organizations. A skilled, dedicated team with a shared passion for SEO could make a significant impact on SEO efforts.

Successful SEO teams have well-defined roles and responsibilities, regular training, ongoing communication and collaboration, and recognition for success. Additionally, the team should have access to enterprise-level tools needed to manage SEO campaigns effectively.

Avoiding Pitfalls and Challenges:

Larger organizations may face some unique SEO challenges like website hierarchy issues, multiple websites, and creating quality content. However, with careful planning and execution, these challenges can be mitigated.

To avoid these challenges, larger organizations must have a well-rounded and skilled SEO team that communicates effectively with other departments. Further, the organization should establish clear goals, maintain brand consistency, and use enterprise-level SEO tools to manage SEO campaigns effectively.

Conclusion:

Large organizations face unique challenges in developing and executing a successful SEO strategy. They must deal with multiple websites, coordinate with various departments, ensure consistency across brands, measure ROI at scale, and build a strong SEO team and culture, among others.

Despite these challenges, larger organizations can achieve the desired SEO results with a centralized SEO management approach, coordinated efforts across departments, enterprise-level tools and resources, measurement of campaigns, and building a strong SEO team. By following the best practices outlined in this chapter, larger organizations can create a vibrant, dynamic, and unified SEO strategy that succeeds at scale.

CHAPTER 15:
INTERNATIONAL SEO

As the world becomes more connected than ever before, businesses are expanding their reach across borders and tapping into global markets. International SEO is the practice of optimizing your website for search engines in different countries and languages so that your content can be easily found by a global audience.

Differences between global and local SEO

When it comes to global SEO, there are some fundamental differences to keep in mind compared to local SEO. For instance, keywords are not always the same from one country to another. That's why conducting thorough keyword research for each targeted country is crucial. You also need to pay attention to the cultural differences and business practices of your target market.

Geo-targeting and language targeting

One of the primary considerations for international SEO is how you are going to target the right audience in different locations. You can start by using geo-targeting techniques such as country-code top-level domains (ccTLDs) or subdirectories. You can also use hreflang tags to specify the language and country of your content, which helps search engines direct users to the appropriate version of your webpage based on their location and language settings.

Country-specific domains vs. subdomains

Choosing between country-specific domains and subdomains is another crucial decision when it comes to international SEO. If your brand operates in several countries with different languages, you might have a better chance of success with country-specific domains. However, if you are targeting different languages within the same country, having subdirectories could work best.

Cultural considerations in keyword research and content creation

To successfully engage an international audience, it's imperative to consider the cultural differences of your target market. You must also understand the cultural nuances when it comes to language usage in your keyword research and copywriting process.

International link building

Link building is an essential aspect of SEO, and it's crucial for boosting your website authority in different countries. You can start by reaching out to local websites and bloggers for opportunities to collaborate or guest post on their platforms. You can also participate in local events or sponsor content with local partners to help build your reputation in foreign markets.

Currency and pricing considerations

When expanding your business globally, you must pay attention to pricing and currency exchange rates. If you are selling products or services globally, you might want to consider localizing your pricing strategy based on the local currency as well as the purchasing power of your target market.

Legal and regulatory compliance

Adhering to the legal and regulatory requirements of different countries is crucial for building a trustworthy brand internationally. You must ensure that you are following local laws and regulations for data privacy, advertising, and any other legal requirements that could vary from country to country.

Measuring success in international markets

Measuring the success of your international SEO efforts is just as important as conducting thorough research and strategy development. Tracking your performance metrics such as ranking position, traffic, conversion rate, and revenue is the most effective way to measure the effectiveness of your international SEO campaigns.

In conclusion, international SEO is a complex process that requires careful planning, research, and strategy development. When executed effectively, international SEO can help your business reach new audiences, drive traffic, and generate revenue in foreign markets. Understanding the nuances of international SEO can help ensure that you expand your business successfully across borders.

CHAPTER 16:
BLACK HAT SEO

Search Engine Optimization (SEO) is an important aspect of digital marketing that enables businesses to rank higher on search engine results pages (SERPs) and drive more traffic to their websites. However, some people use unethical tactics to game the system, known as "black hat ", SEO, in an attempt to gain an unfair advantage over competitors. This chapter will discuss the ethical considerations surrounding black hat SEO and the risks and consequences associated with engaging in these practices.

What is Black Hat SEO?

Black hat SEO refers to any unethical, manipulative, or aggressive tactics used to improve search engine rankings in a way that contradicts search engine guidelines. The objective of black hat SEO is to manipulate search engine algorithms in order to artificially increase a website's ranking and visibility.

Common Black Hat Techniques

There are many black hat techniques, including spamming, cloaking, keyword stuffing, hidden or invisible text, and others. These tactics are designed to deceive search engines into thinking a website is more relevant and authoritative than it actually is, resulting in a higher search engine ranking.

❖ Spamming: Spamming refers to the practice of sending

large quantities of unsolicited emails and messages to people in an attempt to promote one's website. It is done with little or no regard for the quality of the content being promoted or the relevance of the audience.

❖ Cloaking: Cloaking is a black hat technique that involves the use of deceptive coding to present different content to search engines and users. The aim is to fool search engines by showing them a different version of a website than what users see, which results in a higher ranking on SERPs.

❖ Keyword Stuffing: Keyword stuffing involves the overuse of keywords in website content, meta tags, and other text elements in order to achieve a higher ranking on search engine results pages. This tactic can damage the user experience by creating awkward or irrelevant content that detracts from the quality of the site.

❖ Hidden or Invisible Text: Hidden or invisible text is a black hat technique that involves using text that is hidden from visitors but visible to search engines in an attempt to manipulate search engine rankings. This is often done by using font colors that match the background or using CSS to make text invisible.

Risks and Consequences of Black Hat SEO

Although black hat techniques may work in the short-term, they are not a sustainable long-term SEO strategy. Search engines are constantly scanning websites for content that violates their rules, and penalties for violating these rules can be severe.

Search engines have algorithms in place that identify and penalize websites that engage in black hat SEO tactics. These penalties can range from minor drops in ranking to complete removal from search engine results pages, which can have a significant impact on online visibility and traffic. In addition to affecting the website's ranking, these penalties can also damage the website's reputation, brand, and customer base.

How to Identify and Avoid Black Hat SEO

One way to identify black hat SEO is to monitor search engine rankings for sudden or unexpected changes. Unnatural spikes in traffic, sudden decreases in click-through rates (CTR), or drastic changes in website ranking can be indicators of black hat techniques. Websites should perform regular SEO audits and ensure that their content and optimization strategies comply with search engine guidelines.

Ethical Considerations in SEO

SEO should always be conducted in an ethical and responsible manner. Businesses should prioritize creating high-quality content for human readers, rather than for search engine algorithms. There are a number of ethical concerns that businesses should be aware of when engaging in SEO:

❖ Transparency: Businesses need to be transparent about their SEO tactics and practices. This includes communicating with customers and stakeholders about SEO activities and being honest about what they are trying to achieve.

❖ User Experience: Businesses should prioritize creating a positive user experience and providing valuable content to their website visitors. This means avoiding tactics such as pop-ups, hidden text, and spamming that detract from the website's quality.

❖ Reputation: Black hat SEO can damage a business's reputation and brand. This can lead to a loss of credibility and trust among customers.

The Importance of Building a Strong Brand

A strong brand is essential in achieving successful and ethical SEO. A strong brand can help businesses establish themselves as authoritative and trustworthy, which can in turn improve their search engine rankings. By building a strong brand, businesses can attract high-quality incoming links, which can improve their website's authority and relevance in the eyes of search engines.

Conclusion

In conclusion, black hat SEO is unethical and can result in severe penalties for businesses. It is important for businesses to be aware of the risks associated with black hat SEO and to adopt ethical practices that prioritize creating high-quality content and a positive user experience. Building a strong brand can aid businesses in achieving long-term sustainable SEO success that complies with search engine guidelines.

CHAPTER 17: SEO AND OTHER MARKETING CHANNELS

SEO is just one of many digital marketing channels available to businesses today. While it's important to build up your website's organic search visibility, it's also important to consider how SEO fits into your overall marketing strategy and how it can be integrated with other marketing channels.

Paid Search Advertising (PPC)

Pay-per-click (PPC) advertising is the practice of buying ad space on search engine results pages (SERPs) and other websites, and paying each time someone clicks on your ad. With PPC, you can target specific keywords and demographics, and you only pay when someone actually clicks through to your website.

While PPC can be expensive, it can also provide quick results and complement your SEO efforts. Use PPC to test specific keyword combinations, promote seasonal or time-sensitive offers, and target specific audiences.

Email Marketing

Email marketing is the practice of sending marketing messages and promotions directly to your audience's inbox. By building an email list, you can nurture leads, promote new products or services, and keep your brand top-of-mind for your subscribers.

When it comes to SEO, email marketing can help you drive traffic and engagement to your website. Include links to relevant blog posts or promotions in your emails and encourage subscribers to share your content on social media. You can also use email to ask subscribers to leave reviews of your business on Google or other review sites, which can improve your local search rankings.

Affiliate Marketing

Affiliate marketing is the practice of partnering with other websites or influencers to promote your products or services in exchange for a commission on sales. With affiliate marketing, you can expand your reach and tap into new audiences that you might not be able to reach through your own marketing efforts.

While affiliate marketing doesn't directly affect your SEO efforts, it can help you generate more revenue and build brand awareness. By partnering with reputable websites or influencers in your industry, you can also build backlinks to your site, which can improve your search rankings over time.

Display Advertising

Display advertising refers to the practice of showing banner ads or other graphical ads on websites or social media platforms. With display advertising, you can target specific audiences based on demographics, interests, and online behavior, and increase brand awareness through repetitive exposure.

While display advertising doesn't directly impact your SEO efforts, it can be useful for building brand recognition and driving referral traffic to your website. You can also use display advertising to promote specific products or promotions and retarget customers who have previously visited your website.

Content Marketing

Content marketing involves creating and distributing valuable, relevant, and engaging content to attract and retain a clearly defined audience. With content marketing, you can generate leads, educate your audience, and build brand loyalty over time.

When it comes to SEO, content marketing is one of the most powerful tools in your arsenal. By regularly publishing high-quality, optimized content on your website, you can build authority and relevance with search engines, while also attracting backlinks and social shares that can further boost your search rankings.

Public Relations

Public relations involves building relationships with media outlets and journalists and promoting your brand through earned media coverage. With public relations, you can increase brand visibility, build credibility, and improve your reputation.

While public relations doesn't directly affect your SEO efforts, it can provide valuable backlinks and social shares that can improve your search rankings over time. By building relationships with journalists and media outlets, you can also increase the chances of being featured in high-quality publications that can further boost your brand's perceived authority and relevance.

Social Media Advertising

Social media advertising involves paying for ad space on social media platforms like Facebook, Twitter, and Instagram. With social media advertising, you can target specific audiences based on interests, behaviors, and demographics, and increase brand awareness and engagement.

When it comes to SEO, social media advertising can help you drive traffic and engagement to your website and build social signals that can improve your search rankings over time. Use social media advertising to promote specific products or promotions and retarget customers who have previously visited your website.

Integration and Strategy

When it comes to integrating SEO with other marketing channels, it's important to think strategically. Your goal should be to create a comprehensive marketing plan that leverages each channel's strengths to achieve your overall business objectives.

For example, you might use SEO to attract traffic to your website, content marketing to engage and educate your audience, email marketing to nurture leads and generate sales, and social media advertising to build brand awareness and drive engagement.

By combining these channels in a strategic way, you can create a holistic marketing plan that maximizes each channel's potential and delivers meaningful results. Whether you're a small business owner or a marketing professional, it's important to think beyond SEO and consider how it fits into your broader marketing strategy.

CHAPTER 18: SEO CAREER PATHS AND OPPORTUNITIES

In the ever-growing digital world, Search Engine Optimization (SEO) has become an essential component for businesses of all sizes. It is an in-demand skill that has seen steady growth in the job market. If you are interested in a career in SEO, there are many career opportunities available, both in-house and with agencies—one just needs to know where to look and what skills are required.

In this chapter, we will discuss the various career opportunities in SEO, the requisite skills and certifications, industry trends and forecasts, and how to build a successful SEO career.

Career Opportunities in SEO

SEO offers a wide range of career options, from entry-level to advanced, in both in-house and agency roles. As businesses are moving online, SEOs are hired to help optimize websites to rank higher on search engines, resulting in increased visibility, website traffic, and revenue. These are the following roles in SEO:

1. SEO Specialist/Analyst - Entry Level

An SEO specialist or analyst role is the entry-level position in SEO. This role is responsible for researching keywords, performing an audit of websites, and working collaboratively with other teams to improve website traffic.

2. SEO Manager - Mid-level

SEO managers oversee the team of SEO specialists and analysts. They formulate and execute SEO strategies, set goals and budgets, and liaise with external agencies.

3. SEO Director/Head of SEO - Advanced

SEO Directors/Head of SEO are responsible for developing overarching SEO strategies that align with the business objectives. They ensure that the SEO team follows the best practices and key performance indicators.

4. In-house SEO vs. Agency SEO

In-house SEOs work full-time for a company, while Agency SEOs work for multiple clients in the agency's portfolio. In their roles, in-house SEOs have more control over SEO strategies and have a better understanding of the company's industry.

Agency SEOs manage multiple clients with dissimilar needs, industries, and SEO strategies. They work with their team to deliver quality SEO services, but agency SEOs have to build relationships, demonstrate expertise, and ensure client retention.

Required Skills for an SEO Career

To pursue a career in SEO, candidates must possess a variety of skills. In addition to strong technical knowledge, advanced analytical and communication skills are necessary. SEOs must have:

- ❖ Technical Skills: HTML, CSS, and JavaScript knowledge, SEO audit, Familiarity with SEO Audit tools (Google Analytics, Semrush, Screamingfrog, Moz, Ahrefs, etc.), website structure and auditing.

❖   Marketing Skills: Understanding of keyword research, on-page optimization, off-page optimization, content creation, link building, social media optimization, and navigation.

❖   Analytical Skills: An SEO professional should have expertise in data analysis, reporting, user behavior analysis, and website performance analysis.

❖   Communication Skills and Teamwork: Effective SEOs must be great communicators, be able to collaborate across multiple teams, and be able to explain SEO tactics to others within the company.

Certifications and Training Programs

Certifications and training programs are also beneficial for SEO professionals. They demonstrate a commitment to continuing education and show potential employers that the candidate has developed a higher level of SEO expertise. Some of the popular SEO certifications are:

❖   Google Analytics Certification

❖   HubSpot SEO Certification

❖   SEMRush SEO Toolkit Course

❖   Yoast SEO Training

❖   Moz Academy

❖   Search Engine Journal Course about Technical SEO

Industry Trends and Forecasts

SEO is a constantly evolving field, with new technologies and trends emerging every year. Some of the significant trends in the industry are:

- ❖ Artificial Intelligence in SEO: AI has revolutionized the way search engines work. From RankBrain to conversational search, AI algorithms are gaining popularity to create a more personalized, responsive user experience.

- ❖ Visual Search: The emergence of visual search optimization has rapidly expanded with the introduction of new technologies like Google Lens. Optimizing for visual search has become a significant trend in the industry.

- ❖ User-Intention Optimization: Google's search algorithm continues to evolve, centering user-intention. Optimizing for user search intent is critical to creating a more personalized and relevant user experience.

- ❖ Voice Search: Today, there are over 4 Billion voice assistants in use worldwide, and 21% of all voice searches lead to a featured snippet. Optimizing for voice search is necessary in an increasingly mobile-first world.

- ❖ Local SEO: The role of local SEO has become even more critical, with more and more consumers searching for products and services online.

Building a Successful SEO Career

To build a successful career in SEO, it is essential to keep up with industry trends, continuously learn, engage with industry peers, and share insights. Some other suggestions include:

- ❖ Invest in Education and Certification: Stay up-to-date with training, certification programs, and courses to stay ahead of the curve and develop new skills.

- ❖ Work with a Cross-Functional Team: Working collaboratively with other teams in marketing, design, analytics, or development enhances the SEO knowledge and capabilities.

❖   Attend Conferences and Networking Events: Attending industry conferences and networking events is an effective way to stay informed, engage with other SEO professionals, and grow your career.

❖   Build a Strong LinkedIn Profile: LinkedIn is an essential tool in job searches and showcasing SEO skills and capabilities to potential employers.

Conclusion

SEO is a versatile and dynamic field that provides a range of exciting career opportunities. It is essential to possess various technical, marketing, analytical, teamwork, and communication skills and have these skills certified. Staying current with industry trends, continually learning, attending conferences and networking events, and building a strong LinkedIn profile can help an individual build a successful and satisfying SEO career.

CHAPTER 19:
FUTURE OF SEO

The world of SEO has evolved dramatically over the years, and the best practices of today might not hold up in the future. In this chapter, we'll discuss the emerging trends and technologies that will shape the future of SEO and the digital landscape.

Artificial Intelligence and Machine Learning

Artificial intelligence (AI) and machine learning (ML) are transforming the way people interact with brands online. AI-powered chatbots, for instance, are handling customer service inquiries in real-time, while sentiment analysis tools are helping companies understand their customers better.

Search engines are also using AI and ML to enhance user experience, which, in turn, affects how brands optimize for search. Google's RankBrain, for instance, uses machine learning to interpret complex queries and match them with relevant results.

SEO professionals need to optimize for AI and ML by enhancing the user experience and personalizing content.

Voice Search and Virtual Assistants

Voice search is changing the way users interact with search engines. By 2020, it's estimated that 50% of all searches will bevoice searches. Moreover, with virtual assistants like Amazon's

Alexa and Apple's Siri, search is becoming less about keywords and more about natural language and context.

SEO professionals need to optimize for voice search by creating content that isn't just keyword-optimized but also answers user questions in conversational language. This includes incorporating natural language questions and answers in meta descriptions and content, which is more likely to appear in featured snippets.

Video and Visual Search

Video and visual search are becoming an integral part of the search experience. Consumers increasingly rely on visuals to find the information they're looking for, which includes images, videos, and infographics.

Google's visual search tool, Google Lens, for example, allows users to take a photo of an object and receive information about it. Video marketing is also on the rise, with YouTube being the second most popular search engine today.

SEO professionals need to optimize for video and visual search by utilizing structured data on their site, optimizing alt tags and image descriptions, and using a video sitemap. Furthermore, creating informative and engaging videos to complement web content may help increase site traffic.

Personalization and Customization

Personalization and customization help improve the user experience by tailoring the results based on the user's search history, location, demographics, and even behavior. This allows brands to create targeted content that resonates with their users.

Google is already using personalization to a significant extent. For example, users who search for the term "Chicago" from New York get different results than users who search for "Chicago" from Chicago.

SEO professionals need to optimize for personalization and customization by creating content that appeals to different user segments, understanding the user's search intent, and leveraging user data to track user behavior and anticipate their needs.

Blockchain and Cryptocurrency

Blockchain and cryptocurrency are relatively new technologies that will have a substantial impact on the digital landscape. These technologies can transform the way users interact with brands, which could influence SEO.

For instance, blockchain can provide greater transparency in the search engine process, ensuring that search results are consistent and reliable. Furthermore, cryptocurrencies could incentivize users to engage with brands online and even encourage user-generated content.

SEO professionals need to optimize for blockchain and cryptocurrency by understanding how these technologies work and how they could be used to incentivize user engagement. With careful planning and implementation, these technologies could lead to a whole new level of search engine optimization.

Augmented and Virtual Reality

Augmented and virtual reality (AR and VR) are poised to revolutionize the way brands interact with users. Brands can use AR and VR to create immersive experiences for users, providing them with a unique and memorable experience.

Search engines, too, can integrate AR and VR to enhance the search experience by providing a more interactive experience. For example, imagine searching for a pair of sneakers and being presented with a 3D model that you can interact with.

SEO professionals need to optimize for AR and VR by creating content that can be integrated into these technologies and by anticipating how users will interact with brands in a more immersive environment.

The Role of SEO in a Changing Digital Landscape

The role of SEO isn't static. As new technologies emerge and change the way people use search engines, the role of SEO will evolve as well. SEO professionals must adapt and embrace these changes to remain relevant in the future.

In conclusion, the future of SEO is exciting and full of possibilities. By staying up-to-date with the latest trends and technologies, SEO professionals can stay ahead of the digital curve and create impactful strategies that remain effective for years to come.

CHAPTER 20: CONCLUSION AND ACTION PLAN

Congratulations! You have made it through all the chapters of this book, and you now have a solid understanding of the basics of SEO. You are now equipped with the knowledge to improve your website's search engine rankings, increase traffic, and ultimately achieve your online goals. But where do you go from here? In this final chapter, we will recap the key concepts and strategies of SEO and help you build an action plan for your success.

Recap of Key Concepts and Strategies

In this book, we covered the importance of SEO and its history, as well as the difference between organic and paid search results. We also explored search engine ranking factors, types of searches, and best practices for SEO. We dove deep into keyword research and shared tools and strategies for choosing and optimizing the right keywords. We discussed on-page optimization, content creation, backlinks, technical SEO, local SEO, e-commerce SEO, analytics, measurement, and tools and resources available. We also covered SEO's relationship to social media, mobile SEO, SEO for small and large businesses, international SEO, black hat SEO, SEO's relationship with other marketing channels, SEO career path, and the future of SEO.

Building an Action Plan for SEO Success

Now that you have a better understanding of what SEO is and how it works, it is time to create a plan of action to improve your website's visibility and earn more traffic. Here are some action items to consider:

1. Set your SEO goals and objectives

Before jumping into actions, it is important to set your goals and objectives. This will help you stay focused and on track. Some common goals include:

➢ Increase website traffic

➢ Improve search engine rankings

➢ Generate more leads or sales through your website

➢ Increase brand awareness

2. Conduct a thorough website analysis

A website analysis will give you a better understanding of where you are currently and where you need to go. Some key areas to analyze include:

➢ Website structure and organization

➢ Keyword usage and optimization

➢ On-page optimization (including meta tags, titles, and descriptions)

➢ Backlink profile

➢ Site speed and performance

➢ Mobile-friendliness

➢ Content quality and relevancy

3. Develop a keyword strategy

Keywords play a crucial role in SEO success, so it is important to choose the right ones. Consider the following steps:

➢ Determine the keywords your target audience is using to search for products or services like yours.

➢ Analyze the keywords your competitors are using.

➢ Choose long-tail and short-tail keywords that are relevant to your business.

➢ Map keywords to pages on your website.

➢ Optimize your pages around your chosen keywords, including in titles, tags, headings, and content.

4. Optimize your website for search engines

Now that you've identified your target keywords, it's time to optimize your website for search engines. Some key areas to focus on include:

➢ Improving website structure and organization

➢ Optimizing on-page elements (titles, tags, headings, and meta descriptions)

➢ Developing high-quality content

➢ Generating high-quality backlinks

➢ Ensuring your website loads quickly

➢ Mobile optimization

➢ Technical SEO optimization

5. Monitor your results

It is important to regularly monitor your results so you can identify areas of success and areas where you may need to adjust your strategy. Some key metrics to track include:

➢ Website traffic

➢ Keyword rankings

➢ Backlink profile

➢ Conversion rate

➢ Bounce rate

6. Make adjustments as needed

Based on your analysis and the results you are seeing; you may need to make adjustments to your SEO strategy. This could involve:

➢ Tweaking your website structure and organization

➢ Optimizing on-page elements

➢ Developing additional content

➢ Adjusting your backlink strategy

➢ Improving site speed and performance

7. Stay up-to-date

SEO is constantly changing, so it is important to stay up-to-date with the latest strategies and trends. Consider:

➢ Reading industry blogs and publications

> ➤ Attending industry conferences and events

> ➤ Taking courses and certifications to improve your skills

> ➤ Joining SEO communities and online forums

Celebrating Successes and Learning from Failures

Keep in mind that SEO is a long-term strategy, and it can take time to see results. Celebrate your successes along the way, such as improvements in search engine rankings, increases in traffic, and improvements in conversion rates. But don't be discouraged by failures or setbacks. Reflect on what went wrong, adjust your strategy as needed, and move forward.

The Importance of SEO as a Long-Term Strategy

SEO is not a one-time activity but a long-term strategy. By consistently implementing SEO best practices, you will see improvements in your website's visibility, traffic, and rankings. And by staying up-to-date with the latest trends and strategies, you can continue to grow and succeed in the ever-changing digital landscape.

Next Steps

SEO can seem overwhelming, but with the right knowledge and strategies, you can achieve success. Remember to keep your target audience in mind, choose the right keywords, provide high-quality content, and continually optimize your website for search engines. By doing so, you can achieve your SEO goals, increase your traffic, and improve your online success.

Final Thoughts

As we come to the end of this book, I want to reiterate the importance of understanding and implementing the basics of SEO in your online business strategy. Whether you're a small business owner, an entrepreneur, or a digital marketer, SEO can make or break your online success.

By following the principles outlined in this book, you'll be able to improve your website's visibility on search engines, attract more organic traffic, and ultimately increase conversions and revenue. From keyword research to link building, from mobile optimization to local SEO, everything covered in these pages is essential for achieving lasting results.

But as with any tool in your arsenal, SEO requires ongoing attention and adaptation. The digital landscape is constantly evolving, algorithms are changing all the time, and new trends are emerging daily. Therefore, it's crucial that you stay up-to-date with the latest best practices and continue to refine your techniques over time.

Remember: Rome wasn't built in a day - nor was a successful online business. But by mastering the basics of SEO and making it an integral part of your overall marketing strategy, you'll be giving yourself every chance at long-term prosperity. Good luck!

ABOUT THE AUTHOR

Ray Goodwin

Ray Goodwin, is the author behind this series of captivating books on Business Development and self improvement, and has left an indelible mark on the field. He was born and raised in the bustling city of London, where he developed a strong work ethic and an insatiable curiosity about the inner workings of successful businesses. Throughout his illustrious career, Ray leveraged his extensive knowledge and experience to help numerous companies flourish and prosper.

His keen insights and innovative strategies has earned him recognition, driving him to share his expertise with others. Ray believes in the power of sharing knowledge to elevate businesses and empower aspiring entrepreneurs.

Ray's dedication to his craft is evident in the numerous books he has authored on business development and self improvement. His writing style seamlessly blends practical advice, thought-provoking concepts, and real-life case studies, making his books invaluable resources for business professionals and novices alike. His ability to distill complex concepts into accessible language has greatly impacted the lives and careers of countless individuals.

Now retired from the corporate world, Ray and his beloved wife have settled in the idyllic English countryside. Surrounded by the beauty of nature, Ray finds inspiration for his writing and indulges in his hobbies.

Ray Goodwin's books continue to serve as enduring guides for those seeking success in the business world. With a wealth of experience and a deep understanding of the inner workings of businesses, Ray's work remains a testament to his passion for sharing knowledge and helping others flourish.